D1086947

Unsolved

Disappearances

(Volume 3)

Gerald Burns

OTHER SERIES BY THE AUTHOR

The Man in the Green Car

Getting into Trouble

Taken by the Lake

Is that Bobby?

Julia returns to claim her son

Margaret Dunbar Uncovers the Truth

The Man in the Green Car

The daughter of a Vatican citizen and worker goes missing while returning home from school. Her disappearance reveals layers of conspiracies against the Pope and a shady deal between a mafia gang and the church that shook the world. The disappearance remains one of Europe's most enduring mysteries.

*

Location: Vatican City

Date: June 22nd, 1983.

Every place has its own dark secrets. The Vatican City, home to the Pope and the heart of the Catholic Church, is no exception. One of the darkest stories to come out of this place involves the disappearance of a 15-year-old girl on June 22, 1983. This case has kept the world on its toes for decades as numerous conspiracy theories have been provided to explain her disappearance. This mystery has been linked to the activities of secret service members, the Italian Mafia, and disturbing views about the existence of an underground Vatican pedophile ring. Yet, no one can say for sure what happened to Emanuela Orlandi on June 22, 1983.

The Disappearance

Emanuela was the second youngest child of Ercole Orlandi, a clerk who worked at the Vatican Institute of Religious Affairs. This institution also served another function as the bank of the Vatican state. The Orlandi family was part of the small group of people who lived within the city walls and had Vatican citizenship. As a result, the children were free to roam the Vatican streets and visit its gardens like it was their backyard. Emanuela's brother described the feeling of living in the Vatican as being in the safest place in the world. That was until tragedy struck.

Members of the Orlandi family remember Emanuela as an obedient young girl full of life and hope. She was a science-inclined student at school, but her passion was for music and playing the flute. At 12, Emanuela enrolled in the Victoria Conservatory at the Pontifical Institute of Sacred Music, where she was taught how to play the piano and flute three times a week. She looked like the model teenager daughter every parent would love to have until the day she vanished.

The day she disappeared, Emanuela went to a nearby market to buy some pizza ingredients for her mother. She asked her senior brother, Pietro Orlandi, for a lift in his car, but he declined her request, which he now regrets. After a brief argument, Emanuela picked up her flute, put it in her bag, and started towards the conservatory for music lessons after school. She was wearing a white T-shirt, denim shorts, and jogging shoes when she left the house that day.

But there was something odd about her demeanor that afternoon. Her classmates at the conservatory noted that she arrived late for lectures, which was quite unusual for her, and she was absent-minded throughout the day. She later asked for permission to return home early before the end of the day's class at 7:00 p.m.

Before leaving the school that evening, Emanuela called her elder sister aside and told her about a man who offered her a job on her way to the conservatory that afternoon. The man who talked to her was sitting in a green BMW car parked in front of the Italian senate.

The job was simple. All she needed to do was stand on the street and hand out flyers for a makeup company having a fashion show the following week. There was a $200 pay attached to the job, which was very decent pay.

Emanuela told her sister that the prospect of working for this makeup company thrilled her, and he was willing to take the job. But on the other hand, her sister was skeptical, advising her to talk to their parents before taking the job. Finally, the siblings agreed to meet later that evening to present the issue before their mother, but that was the last time anyone in the family saw Emanuela.

Emanuela was missing at the dinner table that evening. Her worried parents called the police to inform them about their daughter. An investigation into the case was launched the next day. First, the police interviewed possible witnesses living around the area where Emanuela encountered the man in the green BMW. Then, they tried reconstructing the series of events from the day before from the information collected.

Emanuela had taken the school bus to the conservatory that day, and the distance from the bus stop to the conservatory gate was less than a quarter of a mile walk. This meant that the people who orchestrated her abduction had little time to get it done without grabbing too much attention.

Eyewitnesses recalled seeing a green car parked across the street with the logo of a beauty brand plastered on the back of the vehicle. Police made various efforts to find this car, but they were unsuccessful.

The Suspicious Calls

A day after her disappearance, a local newspaper published an article about Emanuela and included her family telephone number. That evening, they received the first visitor who wanted to speak to them about their missing daughter. He introduced himself to the family as Giulio Gangi, an agent from Italy's SISDE intelligence service. Gangi told them that he had once seen Emanuela through his cousin. Before leaving their home that evening, he promised to help them find their daughter.

Gangi seemed like the perfect man for this case, determined to get to the root of the mysterious disappearance. He combed through major garages in the area, looking for any information that could lead him to the green BMW in question. One of the mechanics told Gangi that he had repaired the passenger window of a green BMW damaged from the inside. Did this damage happen due to a struggle in the car? It was hard to say.

Gangi was able to trace the said car to a remote location in the Balduina. He encountered a woman in the house who refused to answer any of his questions. She angrily rebuked him and asked him to leave her house. Gangi reported his experience to his boss, who warned him never to return to the place. He was taken off the case a week later and given another job to handle. Why this happened remains a mystery.

Two days after Emanuela was declared missing, her family received a call from a teenage boy who identified himself as Pierluigi. Pierluigi informed members of the Orlandi family that he'd seen a young girl in Piazza Navona, an open space in Rome, who looked exactly like Emanuela. He reported that she was playing the flute, mentioned her hair color, and noted the glasses she was wearing. Pierluigi told them that he was with his girlfriend when he encountered this Emanuela lookalike who introduced herself as Barbarella before informing them that she'd run away from home and was now selling cosmetic products on the streets of Rome.

Another caller who introduced himself as 'Mario' called to give his version of events. Mario informed Emanuela's family that he owned a small bar located somewhere between the Vatican and the conservatory. A new customer walked in one day and introduced herself as 'Barbara.' They got talking, and this young girl confided in him and explained her newly acquired fugitive status. The so-called Barbara said she was sure her family was looking for her, but she would surprise them by appearing at her sister's wedding scheduled for June 30, 1983, where she would play the flute. The last detail Mario provided was compelling since only members of the Orlandi family knew about the wedding arrangements. None of these callers demanded a ransom. They only reported their encounter and cut the call.

Police tried following these leads, but they led to nothing tangible. In the meantime, friends and family began printing and posting pictures of Emanuela around the city, hoping that someone would identify and convince her to return home. That was until something happened that changed the course of the investigation.

On the 3rd of July 1983, Pope John Paul II made a statement during a traditional prayer meeting that shook the Vatican and shocked the world. At the time, everyone believed that Emanuela had escaped from home. However, in his first public statement about the child's disappearance, the Pope prayed for the missing child and asked her kidnappers to return her to her grieving parents.

His position on the issue caused an instant uproar as people wondered why he was so sure that the child had been kidnapped. Nobody had considered kidnapping a possibility at that point due to the last two anonymous calls Emanuela's parents had received concerning their daughter's whereabouts. However, everything changed after the Pope's statement that day and Emanuela's abduction became a possibility.

Other questions lingered, especially those brought by conspiracy theorists who believed the Pope was somehow involved in her disappearance. But even in all of these, the Pope could have had just a simple reason for making that statement that day. Emanuela Orlandi and her family members were among the few inhabitants of the Vatican who had citizenship. So it is safe to say that the Pope and the Catholic church felt responsible for her misfortune and needed to speak about it.

Two days after the Pope's statement, the Orlandi family received another anonymous phone call from a man with a strong American accent. He informed them that the last two calls they'd received were from his team members. The man told them that his people had kidnaped Emanuela, and they were willing to release her in exchange for Mehmet Ali Agca, a Turkish man who was serving a life sentence for attempting to assassinate the Pope in 1981. In addition, a couple of news agencies in Italy received letters from an

Anti-Christian organization (Grey Wolves) demanding the release of the same prisoner in exchange for Emanuela. In their other correspondence, they claimed that they were also holding Mirella Gregori, another Italian teenager who went missing 40 days before Emanuela.

The American man remained in contact with the Orlandi family for months. During one call, he handed the phone to a girl who confirmed that her name was Emanuela Orlandi, and she was a science high school student. Emanuela's parents believed that the voice they heard sounded like their daughter's. However, police told them that there wasn't enough proof their daughter was alive. The caller might have obtained that information from her before the abduction.

The American was not done with them just yet. The next time he contacted the Orlandi family, he directed them to the garbage bin in the center of town containing a photocopy of a music sheet

Emanuela had been learning before her disappearance. Other calls came in during the following months that left the police and Emanuela's family scurrying from pillar to post. They found a copy of her school registration car inside another garbage bin in Palazzo Montecitorio, Rome. Another call led them to a cassette that contained the record of a screaming girl who pleaded with her tormentors to let her sleep. Mario Meneguzzi, Emanuela's uncle, told police that the voice in the clip was that of his niece. After a brief investigation, police told Emanuela's family that the audio was from a pornographic clip.

These calls from various mysterious sources were all monitored by the Vatican. On July 19, 1983, a statement was issued that the Secretary of State, Cardinal Agostino Casaroli, would be speaking to the girl's abductors between 10 a.m. to 11 a.m., Italian time to secure her release. The call never came in at the appointed time. He could only speak to them the next time they scheduled a meeting. The conversation between the two parties was kept under lock and key, and no one could get anything out of the Vatican regardless of how much they tried.

Communication with the so-called American man continued for a while until he suddenly announced that the operation to exchange captives was now closed. No one heard from him after that, and his identity remains unknown to date.

One theory accused American Archbishop Paul Marcinkus of being the American voice in the calls. In 2008, the apprehended girlfriend of a gang leader also accused him of ordering the abduction and killing of Emanuela in 1983. Bear in mind that this Archbishop was also listed by David Yallop, a British true crime author, as a possible accomplice in the assassination attempt of Pope John Paul II. However, the police never interrogated him due to these allegations because they had no real evidence to do so.

Unfounded Accusations

During the investigation, various groups came forward to claim responsibility for Emanuela's disappearance. Research carried out by Italian Intelligence Agencies revealed that most of these groups did not exist, or they were quickly created to be used as a front to bargain with the Vatican. In fact, there was never enough evidence to prove that Emanuela was with the Gray Wolves. However, there were accusations that some European countries were using these fake organizations to further their interest in the Vatican. One investigator came forward to point accusing fingers at Germany, claiming that they created the so-called Turkish group to exploit the situation.

Emanuela's brother, Pietro Orlandi, claimed that the Pope once linked Emanuela's abduction to international terrorism during a family's New Year's Eve visit. He insinuated that an international group was responsible for the girl's disappearance and that the Vatican was doing everything to get her back. A few days later, the Pope helped Pietro Orlandi get a job at the Vatican City Bank. Why he felt the need to do so remains a mystery.

It is unclear why the Pope decided to help out the family in this way, but some believe he did it to deal with his guilt since he knew something about the girl's disappearance. But unfortunately, that was the last time Vatican authorities would communicate with the Orlandi family about their missing child.

Theories

On April 24, 1984, a local newspaper printed a front-page picture of Emanuela and her family standing with the Pope. That evening, Emanuela's parents received a call from an anonymous person that suggested that she was being used as collateral damage in a conflict between Vatican authorities and a powerful mafia group.

The story goes that the mafia group invested over $20 million in Ambrosiano Bank, a financial organization that is widely believed to be connected to the Vatican. Less than a year after this investment, the bank transferred over $1 billion into some South American businesses also reportedly linked to the Vatican. They went bankrupt within months, and the mafia group lost its money. Obviously, this loss infuriated the bosses, and they vowed to take revenge.

According to the theory, the group abducted Emanuela to blackmail the Vatican and force them to return their money. It is almost impossible to say how credible this theory is, but what is known is that the Vatican paid its creditors over $200 million to appease them. Unfortunately, that money was not enough to cover the debt. Furthermore, the last part of the payment was a special burial spot for one of the mafia bosses in the Vatican. Enrico De Pedis, one of the gang's top leaders, was put to rest in the Sant'Apollinare crypt in the Vatican, a spot reserved for high-ranking officials in the Vatican. This proved that the deal existed, and there could indeed be a connection to Emanuela.

In 2018, the Orlanid family received an envelope without a sender's name or a return address. The note in the envelope suggested that Emanuela's remains were resting in a spot close to the statue of an angel. What baffled authorities was that the said spot was known to contain the bodies of two

German princesses. The Vatican gave the green light to pry open the grave and check for Emanuela's remains a year later. The shock came when they found the grave empty, raising more questions about the whereabouts of the German princesses. The bones found nearby were taken for analysis that they belong to people who lived in the late 19th century.

More than three decades later, the Orlandi family has no clue what happened to their daughter, and there is little chance they will ever find out.

The End

Getting into Trouble

A family of four embarks on a camping trip in winter and returns without their mother. The neighbors raise the alarm about her disappearance, and an investigation ensues. Police discover many horrid details about the family's past that make the case even more disturbing. Over a decade later, she is still nowhere to be found. A more shocking detail is the terrible end that befell her husband and children.

*

Location: Utah

Date: December 7th, 2009

Looking at her life from an outside perspective, Susan Powell seemed to have it all: a seemingly loving husband, a lovely marriage, and two precious sons. People who knew the 28-year-old lady at the time have described her as hardworking and an overall positive person. Despite working as a full-time broker at Wells Fargo, Susan still found the time to grow her vegetables and cater to her family. Everything seemed fine until she left her home one day and never returned. The resulting investigation would dig up unsettling revelations about the hell she went through at the hands of her unstable husband and his family.

The Disappearance

On the 7th of December 2009, the day-care Susan's children – Charlie (4) and Branden (2) – attended called to confirm why they hadn't been dropped off that morning. After several unsuccessful attempts to contact the parents, they reported that situation to authorities in the area, and police officers were sent to Powell's household to figure out what was happening.

Colleagues also noticed Susan's absence at work that morning and tried contacting her to ascertain if all was well. But, unfortunately, they could never get to her no matter how much they tried, so they too reached out to authorities to register her absence.

When the police reached Powell's household, they found all the doors locked and no semblance of movement inside the building. Fearing that the family members had fallen victim to air or food poisoning, they agreed to break down the front door and investigate further. They found no one in the house. Susan's personal belongings, including her wallet, ID, phone, and car keys, were lying on a side table.

Later that day, Susan's husband, Joshua Powell, mysteriously resurfaced in the house. During interrogation, he told investigators that he had seen his wife the night before her disappearance. However, he claimed that the last he heard from her was when she announced she was going to bed. According to him, he then decided to take his two sons on an impromptu camping trip out in the forest, even though it was winter, and the camping area was in a temperature of between 10 to 20 degrees with light rainfall.

Every detail provided by Joshua Powell pointed toward absurdity. Why did he take his children out of the house around midnight without informing his wife? Who goes on an overnight outdoor camping trip with two toddlers during winter? These questions lingered even though Joshua looked as shocked as everyone regarding his wife's disappearance.

A few days after her disappearance, investigators declined to comment on whether they suspected foul play in the case. Susan's father, Chuck Cox, reported that the last time he heard from his daughter was on the 5th of December when she called to talk to her sisters. According to Chuck, his daughter sounded fine. He also clarified that he didn't think she could just up and run from her current life, leaving her two children with her husband. A Facebook page was created to find her, and it grew to 100 members within three days of her disappearance, yet no one was hearing from her.

A series of strange events followed Susan's disappearance. For instance, Joshua Powell proceeded to empty her retirement account and cancel all of her upcoming appointments. Such moves are only expected in the case of a dead subject. No one had declared Susan dead, yet her husband was already tampering with her money.

A friend of the family named Tim Peterson noted Joshua's lax attitude towards the whole ordeal. He seemed unaffected by the reality of his wife's disappearance; instead, he seemed more bothered with the police searching his stuff for evidence. Joshua arrived at Peterson's front door just days after the disappearance with a terrible windburn on the back of his hands. When Peterson pressed further and questioned him about Susan, Joshua commented that he wasn't actively looking for her because the police were on it.

Tim Peterson and his wife attended the same church as the Powells – The Church of Jesus Christ of Latter-day Saints. Susan had gotten closer to their family after consulting with them about marriage counseling procedures in the church, something Peterson and his wife had gone through successfully. Peterson told reporters that Susan was open to accepting more friends from the church into her home, but her husband's controlling behavior pushed many of them away from the family. She clearly wanted to leave, but something seemed to be holding her back.

The Investigation

Joshua always appeared disoriented during his interviews with investigators. He insisted on having his lawyers present before he would answer any question thrown at him. He claimed that they were trying their best to trap him in the situation by pointing to his windburns as evidence of his crimes. He looked so visibly shaken during one interrogation that he couldn't correctly answer the year he married Susan.

Forensic analysts collected some samples from a couch in the Powells' home for analysis. One sample matched Susan, but another revealed the presence of a male individual in the house. Joshua said he had no idea of any person the sample could match when questioned.

The Powell kids were also interviewed, and their answers brought interesting discoveries. For example, Charlie told police that the camping trip with his father had indeed taken place that cold night and, contrary to his father's claim, his mother had gone with them on that trip, only that she never returned with them. Weeks later, he eventually told his class teacher that his mother was dead.

On the other hand, Branden told his version of the story artistically, the summer after Susan's disappearance. The boys were living with her maternal grandparents when Branden drew a picture of a family camping trip. His art only accounted for three people in the car: himself, his brother, and their father. When quizzed further, Branden revealed that his mother was in the car trunk in the picture. He explained to his grandfather that she had gotten out of the car at some point during their trip and never returned.

Furthermore, investigators collected information from Joshua's work colleagues, who said he had spoken to them about the best place to bury a dead body, a mineshaft in the West Utah Desert. Joshua told coworkers that he was sure the cops would be reluctant to search the area because of its instability and dangerous nature. Police eventually searched those places, but they found nothing tangible. The investigation continued as residents of Utah and citizens of America continued to wonder what really happened to Susan Powell.

To answer this question, we need to dig into the couple's past and unearth everything Susan went through before her disappearance.

Getting into trouble

Joshua Powell and Susan Cox, both children of religious, church-going parents, met at a church function in late 2000. They soon fell in love with each other and began dating within weeks. Six months later, in 2001, the church organized their marriage. Susan was only 19 years old at the time.

Denise Cox, Susan's sister, recalled the beauty of their first month as a married couple with an elaborate public display of affection. Everyone believed they were a happy, perfect couple. However, not one person had an idea of what Susan was getting into.

Susan's family knew nothing of Joshua's past before their marriage. Joshua's mother, Terrica Powell, would later recount the details of his troubled adolescence. He had once tried to kill himself and also threatened to stab his mother with a butcher's knife. She told reporters that Joshua and his brothers had once hurt her by repeatedly pushing and hitting her. Those details pointed to the fact that Joshua was a troubled child indeed. Unfortunately, he was unable to find the help he needed.

Joshua was also known to take pleasure in hurting little animals around the house, including his sister's pets. His violence raged so much that he would physically attack people at the slightest provocation. No one was available to help curtail this behavior until it spiraled out of control.

In 1994, aged 16, Joshua and his siblings endured a messy divorce between their parents. The tumultuous proceedings he encountered in his parent's marriage may have influenced his character as an adult. The divorce stemmed from conflicts about pornography addiction, mental illness, and polygamy. Steve Powell told the court that his wife had been practicing some strange dark magic that involved Satanic worship. Terrica accused him of possessing some occult material and introducing their sons to pornography at an early age. Terrica also claimed that Steve once told her he was planning to marry another wife into the family. The woman he was targeting was married at the time, but that did not stop him from imagining a future with her, even going as far as writing poems and entertaining sexual fantasies with her in his journal. These allegations of pornography obsession would return later in Steve Powell's life and eventually ruin his relationship with his daughter-in-law.

Terrica and Steve Powell battled for custody of their four children. Eventually, Steve won custody of the three boys, and Terrica had to take care of their only daughter, Jennifer. Terrica reported that Steve would subject his children to domestic abuse involving name-calling and spanking.

Jennifer recalled an event that occurred when she was around 12 years old. For some strange reason, her father had taken her on one of his business trips. They lodged in a hotel room for the evening, and at some point, Jennifer noticed him turn on a program that was just pure pornography, completely disregarding her presence. His sons could walk into their father's office and come across pornographic magazines littered around the room.

Before the end of 2001, Susan Cox became Susan
Powell, and the new couple moved into Steve
Powell's Washington residence to save costs and
prepare for a better future. However, when Susan
joined her husband in his parent's house, she had
no idea of the horror that awaited her there. Her
father-in-law was about to reveal his true nature
to her, and no one would be able to save her from
it.

A Master Voyeur

Long before meeting Susan and becoming her
father-in-law, Steve Powell experienced the reality
of living in a broken home. He was raised by his
grandparents, who lived in Idaho, although he
claimed they took him forcefully from his parents.
He told the court that his paternal grandmother
once told him he would never see his mother
again. He recounted to friends a gory detail from
his childhood in which his grandmother warned

him to keep his mouth shut about his current living situation, then proceeded to drop cayenne pepper on his tongue to explain her stance.

Steve attended The Church of Jesus Christ of Latter Saints while growing up with his grandparents. Then, he was flown to Argentina to offer volunteer services for two years. On his return to America, he met Terrica Martin, who worshiped in the same assembly. The two began dating in 1974. Unfortunately, their marriage hit the rocks in the 1990s, and the divorce proceedings kicked off.

After becoming a part of the Powell family, Susan and Jennifer Powell (now Jennifer Graves) became confidantes. Jennifer was the only one in the family Susan could fully open up about her experience living with her father-in-law.

To say that Steve developed an obsession with his son's wife would be an understatement. He became so addicted to having her around that he would throw caution to the wind to accomplish that. This obsession led to countless instances of sexual harassment of the daughter-in-law. In addition, Steve recorded several homemade videos that documented his infatuation with Susan.

In one tape, Steve sits on a bed as he talks into a camera. He says he has just had one of the most erotic experiences of his entire life. He explains to the camera that he just rubbed Susan's toes, saying that her feet and everything about her is beautiful. He goes on to say that he knows she feels it, too; that from what he has read in her journal, she is not naïve.

Later investigations revealed that Steve had the habit of videoing and taking photos of Susan without her knowledge. He secretly made videos of her in parking lots or whenever they went out together as a family. Some videos had him zooming in on her genitalia with inappropriate voiceovers about his fantasies. For example, one video showed Susan organizing the laundry as Steve says, "God, I worship her. She just turns me on." At one point, Steve tries to convince himself that Susan was aware of his voyeurism, and she was allowing him to get on with it.

Steve Powell never missed an opportunity to spy on his daughter-in-law in her vulnerable moments, even in the bathroom or as she undressed. He would go as far as scavenging her belongings to read through her journals. Being an amateur musician, Steve penned down a couple of love songs for Susan and posted them on the internet under a pseudonym.

The West Valley City police would find a locked drawer full of Susan's underclothes and discarded sanitary products. He had either dug them up or stolen them from the trash can to be used without her knowledge.

Sometime in 2003, Steve decided to confess his love to Susan. He thought it was a good idea to tell the son's wife that he was in love with her. The conversation took place during a ride to Susan's parents' house. Steve had his camcorder recording in the backseat, although it didn't capture any of their faces during the interaction. It is unknown whether it was mistakenly or intentionally placed there to record the conversation. However, the audio retrieved from that camcorder is extremely disturbing when you realize it happened between people of the same family.

In the audio, Susan tells Steve that she is considering moving to Colorado to see a different part of America. Steve laughs it off with a "Yeah" and tells her that he has fallen in love with her. He wonders if he is interpreting wrongly and states an instance when they shared a couch, and he felt she was 'extremely aroused' like he was. Susan quips in and says she has no idea where the conversation is going with the conversation. She reminds him of her status in his father as a daughter-in-law. She tells him that she wants to talk to him about the way he kisses her, stating her displeasure with the amorous gesture.

Steve was unconvinced by her words and held on to the belief that Susan secretly wanted to be with him. He wrote in a journal entry, "I am still convinced she loves me and is sexually attracted to me."

Moving away from trouble

Susan finally got her wish and was able to move out of her father-in-law's house in 2004. The young couple moved their things to Utah, where they hoped to start afresh and thrive in a more stable environment. Sadly, that was never the case, as more marital woes awaited Susan in this new environment, a new nightmare in the person of Joshua Powell, her husband.

A year after arriving in Utah, Susan gave birth to their first son, Charlie. Two years later, in 2007, she had Brandon. During these years, Susan endured extremely controlling behavior from her husband. He never consulted her before making any financial decision that could affect the family. It became so terrible that by late 2007, Joshua filed for bankruptcy with $200,000 in unclaimed debts.

Susan contacted an attorney and spoke to him about her husband's behavior. The attorney advised her to make a video to document all of the family's possessions if her husband decides to sell them off. The video shows her moving around the house as she speaks to the camera, pointing at various gadgets such as computers, RC cars, and other equipment worth thousands of dollars. Her sons can be seen playing in the background as she goes about her documentation.

For other information collected by the West Valley City Police department, it seemed like Susan knew something terrible would happen to her. She had been closely watching Joshua Powell, and she felt he had a tendency to hurt her. Investigators gained access to her bank deposit box, which contained a handwritten will, testament, and a saving bond. In addition, coworkers at the bank knew that Susan had a journal at work that her husband could not access.

Susan's notes from her deposited box revealed the turmoil she had endured in her marriage. Most of the arguments with her husband stemmed from their faith and financial marriage. Joshua wanted Susan to start purchasing groceries at ridiculously low prices that were impossible to find in 2008 America. If Susan did not find food at those prices, he would blame her for their financial problems. He also accused her of not feeding the family well. These accusations came from a husband who had been spending recklessly on RC toy cars and other unnecessary gadgets.

He constantly complained about the economy and how he wanted to relocate to another country. Joshua reportedly opened up to her that he was distraught with how the Republicans were treating the economy and the environment. Susan also documented that Joshua threatened to ruin her life and take the children away from her if she ever filed for a divorce. Next to this quote in her journal was the exact date and time Joshua uttered these words.

Another fight that ruined Susan's peace involved a million-dollar insurance Joshua had taken in her name. This prompted Susan to urge future readers of her journal and will to question her death or disappearance with the words, "If I die, it may not be an accident, even if it looks like one." The document addressed Susan's family, excluding her husband, whom she said she did not trust.

And then the tragedy occurred: just as she had anticipated and prepared for a year before, Susan Powell mysteriously disappeared from her home one Sunday evening in December 2009.

The Search for Susan Powell

The community in which Susan and Joshua lived did everything in their power to find Susan before it would be too late. By Christmas that year, the news was everywhere in Utah as family and friends hoped that someone would come forward with information about their daughter's whereabouts. But unfortunately, they still had nothing to work with three weeks later.

Even after being named a person of interest in his wife's disappearance, Joshua Powell traveled over 800 miles to Washington to attend her vigil and help share flyers with residents of the area. Susan's parents had no idea their son-in-law would be turning up for the solemn event, so it was a real shock to find him there with his candle and flowers.

Joshua was initially cooperative with investigators, telling them about his camping trips with his sons. But, as time went on, he stopped being as cooperative and took on a troublesome character. He once failed to show up for questioning just over a week after Susan's disappearance, and even when he did, he declined to answer many of their questions.

They did not know that Joshua was preparing to leave town permanently, just a month after his wife's disappearance. All indicators pointed that Joshua had no planning of hunkering down to find his wife. He finally had his way on January 6th, 2010, when he, with the help of his younger brother, Michael Powell, packed everything out of the Powell's family home in Utah and moved back to be with their father in Washington. The same father had the habit of stalking Susan in her most vulnerable moments.

It is safe to say that the house shared by the family was too crowded at the time. Joshua would return to Utah a couple of times during the first few months of 2010 to renovate and sell it off to prospective buyers. At that point, he was not facing more intense scrutiny regarding his involvement in his wife's disappearance. Susan's parents were becoming increasingly vocal about their daughter's troubles in her marriage and their suspicion of their son-in-law. They told investigators that Susan had indeed contemplated divorce a year before her disappearance, as evidenced by the correspondence in her journal entries.

More information collected from Susan's journal revealed her distaste for her controlling husband. She fully documented all of her experiences with him in the months leading to her disappearance.

It soon became apparent that she'd been seeking out the best way to secure custody of her two sons and protect them from their father in the event of a separation. She also spoke about the possibility of being kidnapped and taken away from them.

The Susan Powell Website

It was basically a battle of narratives at the point in the story. The Coxs were doing everything in their power to show the world who Joshua Powell really was, but Joshua's family was up in arms to battle them with conflicting stories.

About three months after Susan's disappearance, Joshua and his father created a website that they claimed was to assist discovery attempts. However, bear in mind that Susan's family had already launched another website, called the Susan Cox Powell Foundation, established to help women deal with domestic violence in their homes.

A section of the new website by the Powells featured pictures of Joshua and the kids as they enjoyed some of his favorite activities. One image showed them with Susan sitting in front of a campfire during winter, the same activity he claimed he and the boys engaged in the night Susan disappeared. Investigators who visited the site multiple times could not find anything to corroborate his claims until that point.

The exact section lists some of Joshua's favorite pastimes, such as woodwork and photography. Another section of the website promised readers new Susan content occasionally, including photos and videos chronicling her life. Lastly, the reader is informed that the children, who must be protected from the media, now live with their father and his family. The website also claimed that they are in a loving environment full of hugs and wholesome affection.

As 2010 progressed, the posts on the website became increasingly dark, posted solely to paint Joshua as a good family man and slander the Cox family for no apparent reason. The website's publisher wanted readers to believe that her family destroyed her psyche, which might have caused her to leave her current life and seek something better. Posts were fashioned so that Joshua would look like the victim in this situation.

Weirdly, the narrative morphed into something appalling. The writer suggested that Susan had been in love with another man, Steven Koecher, and she'd been planning to elope with him. Steven was living in Henderson, Nevada when he suddenly went missing on December 13th, 2009, just a week after Susan's disappearance. The website cited their close age range as proof of their plans. However, Steven's and Susan's parents have both come forward to dismiss these claims.

The writer also cited their LDS Church membership and the fact that they were both in West Valley City when they disappeared as other factors to explain their connection. Steve and his son claimed that Susan had eloped with Steven to Brazil, where they intended to reside permanently after starting up a new life.

That wasn't all. The Powells further accused Susan of leading a double life while stating that a long history of mental illness, especially one that affected her mother, may have contributed to her disappearance. Joshua said that he started noticing some changes in her behavior in early 2009, and he asked her to visit a psychiatrist, which she refused. On the website, he claimed that the situation worsened as time went on until she started showing signs of her own mother's similar illness. The Powells also asked authorities to go to

Brazil and investigate marriages that had taken place in LSD Church temples in the past year.

Operation Tsunami

Almost two years after her disappearance, authorities still had nothing that could lead them to Susan Powell. By July 2011, they knew they needed to take arcane measures to make a headway with the case. Their brainstorming session led them to initiate Operation Tsunami. They received permission from a judge to trap and trace phone calls coming in and out of the Powells' residence.

Investigators conducted a room-by-room search of the Powell residence. They came across a lot of clutter that slowed their search. Finally, they encountered a breakthrough in Joshua Powell's room, where they found a camera and a bank box containing nine volumes of Susan's journal, which he took with him while moving back to Washington.

In Steve's room, they found lots of cabinets containing a variety of Susan's personal belongings, including her underwear, hygiene products, and nail clippings. They also discovered cassettes and videotapes containing doctored images and private videos of Susan. The investigation also revealed that Steve would sometimes record himself watching Susan's videos he had recorded.

Steve Powell was convicted and found guilty of voyeurism. Evidence against him showed that he also recorded his neighbor's children as they used the toilet or washed in the bathroom. Investigators believed that Steve had something to do with his daughter-in-law's disappearance, but they found no evidence in his home to connect him to it.

Joshua Powell Goes Berserk

In late 2011, just after Steve's arrest and conviction, Chuck Cox and his wife were awarded full custody of the Powell boys – Charlie and Branden. Joshua moved away from his father's house and was given visitation rights to his sons as long as a social worker was present.

On February 5, 2012, the social worker allocated to the Powell family brought Charlie and Branden to visit their father. Once Joshua opened the door, he grabbed the two kids into the house and shut the door, leaving her outside his home. From her account, the social worker claimed she called 911 immediately to report the incident. In her presence, the house exploded and went up in flames.

Investigation into the cause of the fire revealed that their father mutilated Charles and Branden with an ax before he poured gasoline over their bodies and set the house on fire.

Joshua had taken his time to plan out the murder-suicide involving his sons. He started by donating their toys to charity, emptying his bank account, and calling family and friends to say his final goodbyes. Investigators seemed to have little hope of finding the truth about Susan's death. Joshua was the only one who could help them with credible information about her whereabouts from all indications.

There is rife speculation that another person who knew about Susan's whereabouts was her brother-in-law Michael Powell, Joshua's younger brother. The ongoing theory is that Michael may have contributed to her body's disposal without taking part in the killing.

Police soon discovered that Michael had sold his beaten-down 1997 Ford Taurus for a mere $100.

Cadaver dogs were brought to identify the car among the others in the yard. The dog quickly singled out one of the cars, indicating remains of human decomposition in its trunk. Unfortunately, all DNA tests conducted on this vehicle were inconclusive. A year after Joshua's suicide, Michael took his own life by jumping off a roof in Minnesota. Steve Powell himself died in 2018 after serving a jail term for child pornography.

As of today, Susan Cox Powell is still considered a missing person as no one knows what really happened to her the day she disappeared.

The End

Taken by the Lake

One 4-year-old boy goes missing close to a lake in Louisiana. The search for the missing child lasts over a year, with various dramatic points in the investigation. Eight months later, his mother travels and returns home with a boy she claims is her missing son. The truth about the case is only revealed 92 years later when a grandchild investigates her family legend using modern technology.

*

Location: Louisiana

Date: August 23rd, 1912.

The summer of 1912 was sweltering and uncomfortable for residents of St. Landry Parish, Louisiana, especially in an era without air conditioners or fans. During this time, a family decided to go on a fishing trip in the nearby Swayze Lake in Louisiana, a heavily wooded area with more swamp areas than dry land, even in summer. The vacationing team consisted of 11 members, including the patriarch of the family, Percy Dunbar, and his wife, Lessie. The other members of their group were their children and family friends. They didn't know that the trip would change their lives forever.

The family arrived at their cabin on August 23rd, 1912, and the cleaning exercise began in earnest. Lessie Dunbar busied herself with the preparation of a healthy meal for the family while Percy Dunbar strolled away from the cabin to attend to some work-related matters, much to the frustration of his little son, Bobby, who wanted to go along with him but had to endure a denied request. In a tantrum, the 4-year-old tugged at the strap of his straw hat until it came undone.

A while later, Lessie announced to the group that she would need some fish to prepare dinner that evening. Paul Mizzi, a member of the vacationing party, volunteered to get some from the nearby lake. Bobby again expressed his desire to go with him, and his mother let him go this time. It is important to note that Paul was a trusted friend of the family who used to take Bobby and his young brother, Alonzo, horse riding. The two had become so close that Paul came up with an affectionate nickname for him, 'Heavy.' They picked up their tools and left for the lake.

Later that afternoon, Lessie called the party back home for lunch. The details of their journey back to the cabin appears to be fuzzy, but this was the point Bobby went missing. Paul reportedly claimed that he saw Bobby walking home with them as the two taunted each other playfully like they usually did. They only got to realize his absence after reaching the family camp. Lessie Dunbar raised the alarm, and the men in the group retraced their steps back to the lake to find Bobby. They yelled his name and called out to him but got no response. The party searched all around the woods for hours but couldn't find him. Percy Dunbar returned home to find his son was missing, and he too joined in the search. By nightfall, Bobby was still nowhere to be found. It was the start of a mystery that would hunt many families for years to come.

The search for Bobby begins

Searchers arrived the following day and began exploring the area, searching for any sign of the young boy. With the aid of dynamites, they blasted the water surface, hoping to catch a glimpse of the lake's bottom to see if Bobby was there. Then they used cables with hooks to sweep through the lake to drag his body out of the water. Their effort remained fruitless.

Later that evening, divers entered the lake to search through nooks and crannies where they believed Bobby's body could have gotten trapped by seaweeds. Their search effort only resulted in discovering deer bones, most likely killed in the alligator-infested lake. The searchers also cut up some alligators in the hopes of finding his remains inside any of their bellies. Two days after his disappearance, they still had nothing.

Mrs. Lessie Dunbar suffered from the emotional trauma of losing her toddler. She soon fell ill and returned home to Opelousas, Louisiana, with her younger son while her husband and their family friends continued the search.

A few days after Bobby's disappearance, searchers found a set of footprints leading toward a railway bridge on the other side of the lake. They began considering the possibility that the boy was kidnapped by some of the stragglers that had passed through the area. Some of the searchers had reportedly seen some while working close to the bridge. Could it be that one of them picked Bobby after he wandered away from the fishing party? Their fear was confirmed when the search team found Bobby's straw hat close to the lake. It became apparent that something terrible had happened to the boy. They speculated that someone could have taken him and escaped a boat while the other members of the fishing team were busy with other activities on their way back to the cabin.

The following week, on August 26th, 1912, Bobby's parents reported him missing to the police in New Orleans. Percy Dunbar reportedly printed and sent 1000 flyers with his son's face and plastered them all over town. A local postcard production company assisted in the search by printing pictures of Bobby's face on their postcards to raise awareness about his disappearance. The inscription on the postcard described Bobby as a 4-year-old boy with round blue eyes and light fair hair. His left foot had been burned as a baby, leaving a scar on his toe.

The Dunbar family's friends still hoped that their son would return to them someday. His family and other friendly residents of the town contributed a $1000 reward for anyone with credible information about his whereabouts. The quote attached to the reward stated that the money would be given to anyone who could return Bobby Dunbar to his parents. $1000 was a fairly huge amount for a reward in 1912, amounting to around $20,000 in today's money. Other town residents who knew the family also contributed an additional $5000 to the reward money, bringing the total to $6000. One psychic came forward to volunteer her skill in the hunt, but the effort proved fruitless.

That reward money stayed unclaimed for over a year until Percy Dunbar decided to return all of it to the families who contributed to the cause.

Within that period, Percy traveled to various orphanages in Louisiana. One promising lead took Archie Dunbar, Percy's brother, to Poplarville, Mississippi, after hearing that someone had seen a young boy matching Bobby's description. But unfortunately, Archie returned home with unfavorable news. The boy wasn't Bobby.

Is that Bobby?

In April 1913, Percy Dunbar and his wife received a telegram that informed them about a Bobby sighting in Columbia, Mississippi. The sender mentioned that one man named William Cantwell Walters had been seen in the area with a boy bearing features that matched Bobby's. Because his feet were covered in grime when they found him, they couldn't confirm his identity until his parent's arrival.

William Walters, the child's guardian, had various conflicting stories about his relationship with the boy. First, he told people that he was the boy's father before later claiming that he was only the uncle. Residents around the area could only detain him after they caught him whipping the boy for a minor offense.

Photos of the child were taken and sent to the Dunbar family for them to confirm his identity as their son. When Lessie received them, she opted to travel to Mississippi to see the boy for herself. Apparently, the photos were not enough to conclude.

The boy in question indeed had features that matched Bobby's, with a mole on his shoulder and a scar on his toe. The strange thing was that he never answered the name 'Bobby' and refused to interact with Lessie like a toddler would interact with his mother. He had been missing for close to a year, so one can assume that the separation may have affected his memory of his family. Lessie cried at the scene and told the people that she couldn't confirm that the boy was her son.

Lessie asked to see him one more time the next day before leaving for home. This time she asked if she could bathe him. She believed the activity would help her memory. She reportedly exclaimed while bathing him, "Yes, this is him. This is Bobby, my boy," before fainting in excitement. The boy, too, experienced a change of heart and agreed that Lessie was his mother. Lessie returned home with her son, although some remained uncertain about his identity.

But William Walter had a different opinion. He was adamant that the boy was not Bobby, claiming that his real name was Bruce Anderson. Walter was insistent that the boy was the illegitimate son of his younger brother and his mistress, Julia Anderson, a lady who was once tasked with taking care of their parents. A quick investigation revealed that Julia Anderson was a real person who once worked as a field hand for the family while caring for Walter's parents. Walter's story was that Julia gave him the boy in February of 1912 to embark on a journey with him to see his sister for a few days. Julia reported that she never knew Walter would hold on to the boy for more than a few days. She never saw her son for months after their journey.

Indeed, there was skepticism regarding Walter's decision to take the boy from his mother and never return him as per their agreement. Others wondered if he was using Julia as an alibi to save himself from the punishment of child abduction, a capital offense in Louisiana at the time. As a result, Walter again sent a letter to the Dunbars, pleading with them to reconsider their position about the boy being their son.

Julia returns to claim her son

A few weeks before his trial, Walter asked the
court to arrange for Julia to travel to Mississippi
to see the boy and identify him as her son. Julia
was soon on her way to perform the assignment a
few days later. But there was one problem. Most
residents of Opelousas had accepted Bobby as the
boy who went missing over a year ago. There
were reports of a welcome party that was
organized for him the day he marched into town
with his mother. Julia already had all factors
against her because there was no way family and
friends of the Dunbars would allow her to take
their son.

The boy did not react positively when he met
Julia, similar to how he treated Lessie when he
met her. Lessie and her husband had begun
spoiling him with several gifts, so there was a
possibility Bobby was still reeling from the
excitement of a better life. Also, Julia initially had

a little problem identifying Bobby as her son. That singular detail significantly reduced her chance of getting her son back.

The press covering the case demonized Julia as a single mother with three children from three different men, a poor image for any woman living in that era. Some publications referred to her as a prostitute who couldn't identify her son or care for the rest of her children. In addition, there was the fact that Julia had lost all her kids to various circumstances within the space of three years. She had put up her first child for adoption, and another baby had died from a brief illness. Her only remaining child was this boy that both families were tussling over. Before Julia left the town for her hometown, a court ruled that the boy was Lessie's son, so she had no other option but to leave him at Opelousas. Walter was sentenced to life imprisonment for kidnapping a minor.

Bobby Dunbar remained with his family and grew up to have what can be considered an uneventful life. He met and married a girl when he was 20, they had children, and he passed away in 1966, still bearing his identity as the lost and found Dunbar boy.

Margaret Dunbar Uncovers the Truth

For decades, the Dunbars lived with closure regarding the mystery of their son's disappearance. In 1999, Margaret Dunbar Cutright came into the picture and began a fresh investigation into her family's history.

As Bobby Dunbar's granddaughter and an attentive recipient of her family's legend, Margaret soon became intrigued and curious about her grandfather's identity, wondering if he was indeed the person everyone claimed he was. She interviewed any elderly member of the family who cared to answer her questions. Due to the intensity of her curiosity, her father gifted her a scrapbook full of newspaper clippings about Bobby Dunbar's disappearance.

Margaret was lost in the bulk of information this new material provided her. She pored over all the images, articles, references, and testimonies recorded about the case. Something didn't quite sit right with her. The discrepancies in the various accounts provided by different newspapers led her to search for more information. Her intuition caused her to question her grandfather's identity as a Dunbar. Margaret determined she was going to find the truth about this case. The idea of matching DNA samples became an option.

Margaret consulted her great-uncle, Alonzo Dunbar (her grandfather's younger brother), and her father, Robert Dunbar jr., requesting their DNA samples for testing. Members of the

Dunbar family opposed this action and asked Margaret to drop her investigation, but she didn't. The DNA test result revealed that the man everyone knew as Bobby Dunbar was not the child who disappeared that day in 1912. William Walter was finally exonerated in 2004, 92 years . after his wrongful imprisonment.

Margaret's discovery rekindled curiosity about the fate of the real Bobby Dunbar. Some still believe that a wild animal ate him after straying away from his family as they passed through the woods. Others say that he fell into the lake and was consumed by alligators. These are just speculations as there is no evidence to conclude on any of them. It is almost impossible that anyone will be able to figure out what happened to Bobby Dunbar the day he disappeared.

The End

Let us hear your thoughts

If you enjoyed this book, please support Gerald Burns by going over to Amazon to drop a short and honest review. It would be fully appreciated. Also help us in spreading the word in any way possible by getting more people to read this book. It would mean the world to us.

Thank you very much!

Gerald Burns' obsession with true crime stories and the dark psychology of serial killers started on a flight to New York in 2004 while reading a book on the Manson murders. Few months later he read a story about a young waitress who had gone missing after her shift, never to be seen again. She simply vanished.

Since then he became interested in true crimes stories, stories of disappearances and the weird histories of the world. He started writing out about some of these disappearances in magazines and had people send in their suggestions and thoughts about the cases. The interest for this led him to start writing out some of these stories for the enjoyment of other true crime addicts.

You can connect with him on Twitter, Instagram and Facebook.

Made in United States
Orlando, FL
21 November 2022

24850026R00046